Mic Check

Mic Check

An Anthology of Spoken Word in Canada

David Silverberg
Editor

QUATTRO BOOKS

Editor: David Silverberg
Contributing Editors: Allan Briesmaster, John Calabro,
Beatriz Hausner, Luciano Iacobelli
Cover Design and Typography: Julie McNeill, McNeill Design Arts
Cover Illustration: Jogindra Siewrattan, Creative Concepts Graphic & Print
Photo on back cover: DigitalJournal.com

Library and Archives Canada Cataloguing in Publication

Mic check : an anthology of spoken word in Canada / David Silverberg, editor.

Poems.
ISBN 978-0-9782806-5-9

1. Performance poetry–Canada. 2. Canadian poetry (English)–21st century.
I. Silverberg, David, 1980- II. Title: Mike check.

PS8293.1.M52 2008 C811'.608 C2008-901961-X

Published by
Quattro Books
P.O. Box 53031
Royal Orchard Postal Station
10 Royal Orchard Blvd.
Thornhill, ON L3T 3C0

www.quattrobooks.ca

Printed in Canada

Contents

Ottawa

Montreal

Halifax

Introduction

Poetry on stage can hold its own on the page. I've always thought that the best spoken word – employing creative use of language, original metaphors, unforced rhythm – can work well as a text. While spoken word's appeal relies on the stage, its roots as a writing craft should not go unnoticed.

So what is spoken word? Definitions vary, but it often refers to poetry or performance pieces crafted for the stage – words to be spoken. Whether you're talking about ancient Greek storytelling or national poetry slams or lyrical poetry drifting over guitar riffs, spoken word is staking ground in Canada. Thing is, it's not going to find you; as with any grassroots movement, *you* have to find it.

But where do you find the spoken word artistry that will inspire you?

Creating the first anthology of modern Canadian spoken word poetry (no joke, look it up), Quattro Books and I wanted to select a medley of voices and styles peppered across the scene. There's no CanCon theme of choice, no mandate to feature a certain poetry community. It was important to scan coast to coast to find the talents bubbling up from our soil. This anthology presents the new and boldly raw, the wild dreamers with seismic energy shivering through their pens, the philosophers holding in their breastbone three-minute power-poem-ideas. *Mic Check* could be your first adventure into spoken word or it could be your 400th, but the intention remains the same: bring spoken word poetry out of the cafés and pubs and into your hands, your memory, your library.

Because spoken word can also come alive on page.

It's a truism that hit home when someone from the audience at Toronto Poetry Slam came up to me one time and said, "Hey, why isn't there a book of this stuff?" I've wondered the same thing since I started TPS in 2005. The lyrical language is there, the passion is there, but the opportunities to publish are spotty at best. Most poets self-publish their chapbooks. This guy checking out the slam reminded me of how young this community is, and how we're just realizing how working together and bridging provinces can only strengthen the spoken word scene.

Nothing better exemplifies this inspiring community than the annual Canadian Festival of Spoken Word. Every year, Canadian cities send slam teams to this rotating festival, which began in 2004. These slam teams – comprised of five slam poets per venue – blast their perfected poems over three nights, but it's not about the competition. We are hungry to know about other performance poetry scenes across the country, and we're thirsty to absorb different poetic styles, imaginative content, heart-stopping team pieces. There's nothing like a CFSW.

Many of the poets you'll be reading in *Mic Check* come from the CFSW alumni squads. There are legends of spoken word anthologized beside slam poets just dipping their toes in the slam water. As varied as *Mic Check* is, one constant ties these artists together: the honesty poured onto paper. And it doesn't always have to be linear, as Vancouver's R.C. Weslowski shows us. He can veer in unexpected directions in one poem, but he can also come back to a haunting story about his childhood. The unfiltered truths, just a poet and a microphone, just a pen and a pad…it's what makes spoken word poetry so impacting and unforgettable.

Speaking of unforgettable, there's something about Magpie Ulysses' "Killing Fields" poem that never fails to send chills up my frontal lobe. Its blunt description of a night home from blood-soaked work conveys Vancouver's Downtown Eastside without ever leaving the dreamy thoughts of a woman crawling into bed with her lover.

But would it be scarier to wake up in a relationship to find you've become a hotel? No, it's not an existential question but the subject of "24-Hour Heart" by Barbara Adler, who can infuse sweeping rhythms into pitch-perfect verse like it's second nature. She can take a common experience such as lust and turn it into an original metaphor you'll want to bookmark for future reference, if only to remember how everyday life can be poetry in motion.

Moving east, Calgary is home to a couple poets anthologized in *Mic Check* who deserve national attention: Moe Clark brings the tragedy of cultural suicide into language both accessible and heart-wrenching, and she unknowingly offers a pithy quote that excellently sums up the purpose of this anthology: "There's no time like the present/ to speak up and/ be heard."

Reading Shone Abet's "Queer Girl" is empowering for its message of gender-bending independence. There's a spice-sprinkle of moxie through the poem, reminding us that standing up for one's individuality deserves a bold voice that is both strong and intelligent.

Sometimes, honesty can be funny. Like in how Skip Stone from Winnipeg perfectly summarizes the time-honoured tradition of playing Nintendo for hours. If Bowser, Duck Hunt and a black cross control are familiar terms, then "8-Bit Villain" is a shot of nostalgia or a stark reminder of many sleepless nights fighting bosses.

"Stop doing Reiki on me!" I know, it sounds like a non-sequitur but it's the title of Andrea von Wichert's anthologized poem. A critique of a Reiki practitioner's aggressive tendencies turns into a comical conversation you'd hear between frustrated friends. Von Wichert has a knack for dialogue and the back-and-forth poem carries its own momentum that truly comes alive on the page.

Other times, honesty can be soulful. If this is your first time peeking into Amanda Hiebert's soul via her poetry, I envy you: You have a lot of memorable poetry to discover. When I first heard Amanda perform in Toronto several years ago, I thought: *This is poetry that can carry its weight on paper.* She has a talent for describing people without cliché, without mincing any words. Read "Farm Grandma" if you've ever wondered how a woman's fall from grace can sound tragically beautiful.

Not far from Amanda's knack for characterization is Valentino Assenza's talent to craft poignant love poetry like he's simply breathing it out of him. In "Let Me," he wants it all – the bliss, the passion, the wet sheets and the spinning night of love's daze. And like Val's performance voice, the poem's tone is dripping with undeniable conviction.

One of the most difficult spoken word tricks o' the trade is timing, and Mike Smith is an expert in comedic timing. In "Advertising," for example, he inserts italicized asides at just the right moments, often when you least expect them, thereby adding a second voice to a personification piece already doused with humour. And don't be fooled by the jokes – Mike is one of the best writers in the spoken word scene today, and he has a talent to express what is often inexpressible.

Portraying the Toronto spoken word scene wouldn't be complete without including L.E.V.I.A.T.H.A.N. This hip-hop-tinged poet is a sight to behold (if you like tongue-twisters, you'll like Levi) and his messages resonate powerfully on paper, too. Read "Cars" to learn why a L.E.V.I.A.T.H.A.N. piece stays with you long after the final breath.

Also spicing his work with a hip-hop flavour is Ritallin (a.k.a. Greg Frankson), an Ottawa poet who co-founded the Capital Slam. A piece like "Feel the Old School" brings us back to the golden days of hip-hop, and he name-drops several major influences on today's spoken word poets. His poems are just a taste of what this artistic influence has in store for the rest of Canada.

Spoken word has developed into many sub-genres, and one of those is the "list poem," whereby each line begins similarly. Such is the case in Kevin Matthews' "Give it 2 me," which feels like Dr. Seuss doused with Ginsberg. Matthews infuses the poem with a playful tone, such as in the line "i'm taking chances with phonetically transmitted diseases/ i'm taking teenaged girls – on shopping sprees."

I first met Kaie Kellough in Montreal when he performed with my spoken word troupe, Last Call Poets. His dub style coated his words with fluidity instantly attractive to the ear, and his poetry in *Mic Check* displays those same qualities. In a poem like "vox versus," it's almost hypnotic to let the inner ear sway to Kaie's rhythm and unorthodox poem structure.

Finally, the East Coast is well-represented by Ardath Whynacht, a punchy poet whose traumatic experience in "Sliding" reminds us where to lay our priorities. Also, in another poem she writes: "Maybe this whole spoken ritual is just about uncovering secrets." And maybe this *Mic Check* anthology is a way for you to peek into those secrets to see what's boiling beneath these poets' skins.

Looking at the roster assembled in *Mic Check,* it's hard not to feel good about the state of spoken word in Canada. The talent is truly inspiring, and these poets represent the tip of the iceberg, for two reasons: first, many of these artists are quite young and their best days lie ahead. And second, these spoken word phenoms are a sampling of what Canada has to offer in this budding art form. One of the most difficult tasks in editing *Mic Check* was selecting the poets; if I had my way, the anthology would be three times longer and include an encyclopedia of spoken word artists that deserve your attention.

But these 15 artists should get you started. And it's the intention of *Mic Check,* as it is the intention of almost every poetry slam and spoken word event in the country, to let a few words spark your curiosity to seek more, to find out what other artists are carving new ground in Canadian poetry. You don't have to look far; communities across Canada are home to spoken word talent just waiting to be discovered, from Durham, Ont., to Kelowna, B.C.

I welcome you to dive inside the world of spoken word and get excited. You won't regret it…and you will wonder where this poetry has been your whole life.

David Silverberg

Barbara Adler

Music

There are people who can sing,
as if every morning were the first Sunday.
People born with voices like a holiday
who can hold notes
all the way into the back-then of easy summers.
And it's this kind of musician
who makes me search for things that I could trade in,
just for the ability to sing along;
but I was born with the wrong gifts –
vocal chords that stretch like city-line limits.
I don't like to sing much in public
so I've learned how to keep quiet in the mix.

But lately, I've been playing the piano again more often.
And it's mostly this private kind of awful;
the musical equivalent of those legendary little old ladies
who knit tea cozies for their dogs
and who nod and smile sagely
whenever art history enters the conversation –
even though we all know their favorite Genre of Painting
will always be
Kittens-in-a-Basket-ism.

The kind of Art that seems to say:
"meow meow meow
meow
meow
meow."

And this is the kind of easy
that is simple to snicker at in your 20s –
the age of irony so ironic
it has to point itself out as being irony.
But somehow,
despite this disability

I managed to hear the story,
of how, when the musical scales were being standardized in
European monasteries,
monks would be lined up in a row.
And starting at the low bass they all sang
as far as they could go in their range,
until they reached the highest note in the scale
each pitch matched to a monk
so that according to this story,
C, or "Do,"
is really Joe Monk from hundreds of years ago,
singing at his limit,
or rather setting it,
as if just by being yourself you could be perfect.

And there are some lucky souls
who spend their whole lives knowing this kind of bliss;
but my mantra has always been:

please, make fun of me,
I'm insecure, and I like the attention.

So it doesn't get much more mind-blowing than this.

But there's another story,
of babies who cry in key and howl in harmony
to everyday household noise.
Who grow up as Ella Fitzgerald girls and Mozart boys,
cupping the whole mythology of talent
in their ears.
They can sing, and hear, and name any note
perfectly.
And apparently, we are all born with this ability
but, lacking training,
we lose it with age.
And even though it has been proven that a perfect ear
is no gage of a musician's future ability –
there is something like a first Sunday
in the way we will always be stretching
to the might have been ours,

but now can never be:
like an easy holy night
our faces stark like black and white photographs
so we flirt with echoes to hear our own names shouted back,
but even that silence is simple math
when we realize that what we hear as a note
is simply speed,
a string vibrating
doubling in frequency
until our ears reach their limit
and hear one constant pitch,
if we move fast enough
we become music.

But there are some cathedrals whose spires are talent tipped,
while we are the Velvet Elvis of raw-lipped voices
wondering simply if we can be good enough
to make someone happy.
Hoping there is some value in easy softness pressed to its limits,
so when we find something we can give,
we double it
and submit to the holy halls of our love despairs
where walls are gapped
like finger cracked arpeggios,
our mouths close around the pass\fail certainty
that judgment day
really is a set of scales.
And no matter how well we are hiding
we will be singled out to sing
more tests even in death lining breath after breath in a row
always behind and below, sighing
dear black and white keys
please raise me
to bodies that were born too slow,
but that can double it
and fly quick on tongues that are really capes,
the great escape breaks the last vocal chords
bound to the lord's prayer, we are not player pianos
moved most by ghostly deeds,
we chose the worship of souls

too speedful for their bodies,
we chose our own stage sacrificing deities, born perfect
but losing it quickly
in border skipping jubilance
yelling molto meno kittens in baskets!
Assai velvet, and poco tie-dye!
Allegretto and pui vivace
joyful joyful Sunday

When the second-to-last monk in the line up was called to sing,
his tongue, teeth,
and that little round thing at the back of his throat
all grew about four sizes too big.
And he could swear he smelled the blackberry brambles
outside the chapel window fermenting to blood,
and he thought:
Any minute now,
I'm going to have a giggling fit.

But he did sing.
And when it was done, he said:
I'm sorry that wasn't better.
But I have a whole army of sagely nodding little old ladies
standing behind me,
saying
happiness is still that voice
walking too briskly to where the river lies.
It isn't time yet for the holiday
but we try.

Barbara Adler

24-Hour Heart

My love
one morning I woke up beside you,
and found I'd become a hotel.
I was wearing a neon sign around my neck,
and when I reached down for my heart,
I found my rib-cage neatly boxed into sections.
And in each one there was a bedroom.
And each bedroom had one bed, and no bathroom.
And there were frisky teenagers trying to lose their virginity in B6,
and 5 men in the lobby trying to mooch smokes from the mousy
  receptionist.
And on the landing to the fourth floor
a stag-ette was vomiting something pink,
while one staircase above, her bored beefcake stripper flexed and
  reflected his tan
in the plastic framed print of a Renoir painting.
I took it all in, but I didn't panic.
The sign around my neck said:
Your 24-hour heart is constant/constant /constant/
and I thought, Shit –

maybe I've always wanted to be a hotel.

My love
one day while you were dreaming, I woke up
and found I'd become the kind of establishment
where musicians came from miles around to die.
An elephant graveyard full of midnight snack philosophers,
and damp people curling at the corners like the scraps left by
  cookie cutters,
all soaking chemical regrets.
I examined myself,
and judging by the stains on the carpet,
my life comes equipped with four-and-a-quarter ghosts.

Jesus fish on bed posts winked dirty at the peep holes in the showers down the hall,
where I kid you not
all the little complimentary soaps
were stolen from better hotels.

Okay, I know it looks bad,
but if you were to close your eyes in the shower steam
wafting stolen perfume,
you could pretend you were really Someone.
Someone Special,
like Brooke Shields.

Okay, I know it IS bad,
but I woke up one morning and realized I kind of liked being a cheap hotel.
I got to see everything,
and no one asked for anything but to be seen,
and so I watched.
And in the bedrooms beneath my breastbone,
nervous lovers were circling each other
like child soldiers getting crushes on the enemy.
And at the exact split-second they finally pressed skin,
I checked in on the barroom by my crotch,
and there was a woman.
And she was letting her scarf fall into a stranger's lap like an instant secret.
And when they took the elevator together to her room on the fourth floor,
I got to see how she composed her face for the mirror
so she wouldn't look
so half-assed guilty
like a woman who had planned her own surprise party.

Apparently, everyone in my hotel was completely taken by all things momentary.

And maybe that's why you looked like you felt sorry for me
when I told you all of this.
You said: That doesn't sound romantic.

And I said: You're right.
My heart is not a flower –
it doesn't beat so you can smell compliments.

But if every morning I'm a cheap hotel,
then every evening I turn into a cathedral.
Well actually,
it's an all day all night 365 days a year greasy spoon,
which in my opinion comes down to just about the same thing.
Sign on the door doesn't even say, "Come on in, You're Welcome,"
because that would be redundant.
The sign says:
my 24-hour heart is constant/constant/constant/

So it's full of kids feeling the brave kick of having beat the night,
daring each other to snort petroleum-based cream products –
It's constant/
and full of "just friends,"
"just drinking coffee,"
but anyone with eyes can see that actually
they're breathing prom night punch bowls from the hollows of each
other's necks
until they're too drunk to drive anything
but road sex on a switch-back pelvis –
it's constant/
as the women with faces like pickled lilies smiling sadly but still
smiling
as they take your order.
And you're writing, or just sitting there staring,
but be warned, if you ARE writing, someone always asks if it's
poetry.
And then you have to see their sketchbook.
And usually, it's full of pages and pages of dragons and fairies,
until you come across the one section full of hauntingly realistic
depictions
of your former French teacher having sex with robots –
it's constant/
like carnival sweat
constant/
like milkshake punches and nose laughs

dawn dusk neon
constant /constant/constant

So yes,
maybe some days I wake up with a No Vacancy sign around my neck,
and those days,
it looks like Love is just the name I've written on a bad cheque,
and I leave you alone like money.
But every day when twilight falls
I ache the walls so hard,
the guitar player in room B46 stops arguing with his girlfriend,
and he starts strumming.
And he strums through the racket, and the bad smells,
and all the way into the cathedral evening.
So my friend, comrade, lover in arms
swear, spit, make a toast, clink pelvis on it.
Because if you are willing,
we will take our moments as they flicker under this immortal fickle
  filament.
You see how it is:
on again/off again/on again/off again
but we know this:
even if we go our ways
our 24-hour hearts are lit.

R.C. Weslowski

Love Part 1: The Bun of Disquiet

Love:

Love is the honey country. Where the bun of disquiet
no longer prospers. Where the Mapplethorpe hummus buggies
no longer rule. Love is where the umbrella is upside-down and
open. It now catches rain.

So from the rusted pitch-fork
buried deep in the heart of the garden of syphilis,
to the tambourine moon pump swinging neon in the horn blow

Come.
Come.
Come to this country.
So many are waiting and
YOU are welcome here.

Butter.

How does one get there? What are the sign posts along this road?
That riddle is easy. Just ask the Great Meat Box.
Put the answer in a pansy and mail it to Norway. Count to 10
backwards using the alphabet as a lemon drop.
Practice your punctuation. Throw your bible at the sun.

Good.
Good.
This will never work.

Be impatient with all those who are willing to offer you advice.
They are just trying to make themselves look good
while flogging a pasta envelope. Shut the fuck up once in a while.
Love will come. It always does.
It just might not be wearing the noose you expected.

So how will you know? Well,
this just in from Jotunheimen, Hemsdal and
the Hunderfossen family park 15 kilometres north of Lillehammer.
Upon falling in love you will still feel worthless,
Just a little less desperate. After that
things become increasingly moist.

All previous points of reference are no longer valid.
All former measuring sticks are immediately cropped.
Upon falling in love you will see through a new set of eyebrows.
The world is born anew.
It's kind of like the first time
you hear a kid swear.

Come.
Come.
Come to this country.
So many are waiting and
YOU are welcome here.

Suicide prevention day arrived three weeks too late.

I'm hanging out at the library
as I often do, searching for Brendan McLeod
and loitering in the poetry section
trying to remember Alden Nowlan's name.

I like that guy a lot. Especially
the poem about the bull-moose,
or the one about not letting his son
take a sip of beer at a party and I
really like the story where he visits
a school for the mentally retarded.

So I grab a copy of
I'm a Stranger Here Myself and I
head over to the escalator where
I see a display that says
Suicide Prevention Day is September 10th.

Who the hell schedules these things?
My friend Deanna killed herself
seventeen days ago. If these losers
had been on the ball
at least I could have given her a pamphlet.

As it stands it's like offering
a sex education class three weeks
after the abortion. The pie's been thrown,
the gum's been chewed, the bull's
been gored, the moon's gone full,
the cow's been tipped, the dam has burst
and the dish's run away with the spoon.

And now this is where I'm supposed to say
something profound. To embrace the lessons
learned. Why? She's dead. My heart is broken
and for the first time in months of summertime drought
there's rain. You can tell Fall's just around the corner,
Winter's on its way and I'm doing my best
to ignore this hangover I keep presenting myself with
and still believe in the promise of spring.

R.C. Weslowski

Waterfalls

When I was a boy
my daddy called me "Roundy" instead of Randy.
I was his chubby little buddy, the fat part of father
a boy in a bubble drowning upside down
trying to figure out how round is a round.
Is a "round" round around another "round?"
Is a "round" round around an "around?"
Are a "round" and an "around" round in sound only?

Wheely,
this is a box
with a ring running circles 'round me
'till I'm straight jacket numb
making that bubble grow tighter.

My music teacher put his hands down my pants
when I was six years old. Played with my squeeze box,
stroked on my tuning fork, told me to sing into his.
Songs so discordant they were played on broken keys
again and again and again by others
more accomplished.

I felt like a broken record,
a tired example going
'round, 'round again, spinning
scar upon scar
until my body felt like a mountain
hiding a giant
trying not to be noticed
while constantly bumping into things,
bruising soft like broken fruit
afraid of the touch that touched too much
unwilling to scratch
an already sensitive surface,
feel the shape of the pain underneath.

This is not the body I was given by God.

That's the one I've been trying to find.

The body
that
loves,
that
lusts,

that
wants to fuck,
that
gets an erection,
the body
that
needs
to touch and
be touched
to be tactile and
alive,
to taste and
to smell.

I love the way a woman smells.

A scent that's all peaches and
Jesus
What woman would want to kiss these lips
that have sucked the family cock?
What woman would want to touch this skin
that has been peed upon?
This skin of sin and fingerprints
that folds its self in upon itself
like time after time after time
because time can be a crooked circle
granting the past
a shape
a form

a frame of reference
you know, you know, you no longer fit into
but still can't help but perceiving
blinded by an eye's age
too stubborn, too afraid and too old
to grab hold of
the snowflake full of everything frozen
watch it dissolve in your hands.

But I believe
that out of despair arises
the greatest possibility for love
if we allow ourselves to remain open
when everything inside of us cries NO.

Because the land shape of things
is infinitely patient, waiting
for our spirits to catch up.

Even now the snows of
Kilimanjaro are disappearing
revealing Pantagruel's kingdom
underneath
an undiscovered country
wiping the dust of the dead from its eyes.

The land shape of things is always
forgiving.
Put your ears to my heart
and listen.

Mountains
are digesting themselves
with waterfalls.

Magpie Ulysses

Killing Fields

I come home in the shells
of gunpowder darkness.
It is 4:30 in the a.m.,
and I should be
all glitter and candy floss
slipping in smooth and soundless
next to you in your delicate slumber.
And you should turn to take me,
and taste
cigarettes & lipstick on
these sultry
diva
cabaret
lounge singer
lips.
Yes, this should be
every single middle school wet dream
you ever had,
or wanted to.
This 4:30 in the a.m. should be
romantic.
Instead,
I drop my bike on the back porch,
climb stairs,
take my shoes off at the door.
Red-winded,
from my eyes I peel contact lenses
now stuck to my cornea like melted polar fleece
at a Girl Guide campfire gone terribly, terribly
wrong.
I leave my bag and clothing
at the bathroom door,
turn on the shower,
step into the steam,
and the pipes grumble.

Baby, I'm home from the killing fields,
just let me wash
this blood from my hair
and I'll be right there.
You don't know it,
but I'm in there,
counting the shower tiles
to etiquette school
to take me away from working in this poverty vacuum.
If you don't know what fresh blood smells like,
I can tell you.
It's like the aching dirt under the
fingernails of old leathered cowboys.
Like day-old piss in the stairwells of every
downtown parking garage you've ever been in.
Like dead dogs, wrapped in plastic, laying on the sidewalk,
baking in the Mexican sun.
Like men and young boys,
and the truth of a little cock suck,
like that bitter whisper that tells you to just shut up.
Like a 10 a.m. old man circle jerk
in the cemetery in St. John, New Brunswick,
the horse slaughterhouse at the junctions of highways
like an all night #20.
Fresh blood smells
like puke and alcohol and cologne
on Granville St. on New Year's Eve.
And I watch it all run down the drain.
In the same way a woman's mascara'll
run away on her,
even though
it's not raining.
Like an infection on your heart valve at 20
from too many heroin injections,
the killing fields,
come
home with me…
If only for a flash.
Because I know
that tomorrow begins
in the second I forget them.

This 4:30 in the a.m.
should have been
romantic.
Instead, I sidle in at 5,
and arm over arm you pull me in,
say,
you smell good,
and ask if it's raining out there in the
shells of gunpowder darkness,
to which my only whispered reply
is
yes.

Magpie Ulysses

There Are Flowers

Take my heart
from my throat
and smash it.
I am freaking out.
You see,
the way things seem to want to be
are in a slight shift to the left
and I don't really ever want to
permanently return back
right.
So I drink from the indoor water feature
in my favourite downtown hotel.
I eat drug deals, and dust,
and shade-grown snail mail,
and wait
for what I have always
wished upon a star for.
Which is this:
the moment in which I come
undone in a quiet fury.
Inside, there is no silence in madness.
But sometimes,
it creeps up on you as quietly as sheets to laundry lines,
as the tides wonder of Orcas and gravity,
as her lips moving softly on her death bed,
wondering if she will ever play the grass between her two thumbs
   again.
And madness is as unknowing
as hands that have never moved soil with shovels,
as small breasts in big busted dresses,
as the crows whispering sunset.
I wait for daylight to come
like the embalmer's breath
on open caskets of children killed in car accidents.
I wait to be marked by

the passing of these days that feel like bricks to the teeth.
I want nights spent reminiscing in a wine-soaked bathtub
about that time I lost my shit,
and I never
want to smell the same sweat stain again.
In the minutes that feel like years,
this is the power of an unmarked passage of panic
and the prayer of those that will their boots to stomp traceable
pathways into nighttime mud,
and all the places they will wander,
looking for dark places to hide,
and the stairwells they will seek
to share lustful secrets with.
Inside
the quiet fury is loud, loud, loud.
Says
"lady,
just do it."
Make plans with other peoples' mouths held in yours
so they will never again know a kiss without words.
Steal fruit from the orchards,
hop fences,
fall in love 6 times a week,
open your legs
so they can breathe.
Clean the leaves of trees in city parks
so they can breathe.
Drink far too much whiskey.
Take bouquets to your favourite public steel structures,
kneel down and pray.
Don't wait for the train,
run.
Challenge strangers to races on the steepest of stairwells,
compose love songs for the raccoons.
Take your ambivalence to the imbalances
that prey on you like electro-convulsive therapy on the brain.
Strangle
your
indifference
to

death.
Breathe, breathe, breathe.
We could all spend this life pretending
that we are
slow moving Mississippi river bank picnics.
But there are flowers pressed
to a butterfly screen press
still hopeful for drying in a pour down.
So please,
let my quiet fury take its clothes off in the public fountain
and
wade.

Moe Clark

Tits with Lime

At the bodega
Oh mega five
chicks gettin out
on the loose
& stayin alive
Lipsticks rouge
rouge   rouge   rouge   rouge
Electric smiles
whats the skinny?
martinis: tits with lime
Sublime intervention
on the dance floor
heat to the beat
sweat furrows my brow
Lady Luck   *be a lady*
Partner swing
swig and jig this
shot glass
hot ass
high strappy heels
lacy breasts heave
to the music round
disco ball round
shattered light
spills out and about
our faces
making speed
feeling greed of night
Sexed here
hormonal intervention
invention of heat
meat market place
for pick-up
Dont be shy
grab that boy

wall flower
power of will
power of the
mysterious
feminine
mystique?
Erect barrettes
stand tall upon our heads
raised up high
in beehives
wearin gloves that hide
paper cuts
from sacred work
secularized
communified
Lady Luck *be a lady*
Cross your Ts
dot your Is
and I
look deep into your eyes
across the smoky bar
filled with tongues
sleek and smooth
sipping drinks
toying with the straw
drawing in the silky
taste of gin and ginger
marmalade
What is made and tipped
for the equipped
sinner tonight?
Sinners take flight
screams and cries
between my thighs
this nights last quest
upon my breast
watch it moan
heave up then down
disco ball still spins
brain cells pop

and crack
like these walls
under attack
against the headboard
What happened?
to the (alpha) omega bodega
heat of the night
now I am done
slipping out of sight
bright spirals
through my brain
insanity verges
on this drunken
euphoric
haze
dazey fields
mixed with lazy eyes
this dream?   Nah, real time
takes me back
to the twist of lime
shots in line
straws lost
on the floor
beer wets my
moonwalk pace
the gin
the juice
the sips, spills an thrills…

Lady Luck   *be a lady?*
Now I lay me down to sleep
next to this creep
deep into the
great
intoxication
of that
deviant
smile.

Moe Clark

Expose It

Last year I was at a conference holding the book Métis Survivors of Residential Schools *when the elder woman sitting next to me pointed to a picture of herself on the front cover. I smiled, unaware of the contents in the book. She smiled back, knowing I would soon find out.*

**

You
are standing in a steaming hot room
holding a screaming two-year-old child in your arms,
when all of a sudden harsh sprays of ice-cold water
come streaming over your thin form.
Cries pierce your ears.

Now expose it:

The picture
of anything less than truth,
anything more than ruthlessness.
Expose this:

Have you heard the story of the residential school systems?
Began before the 20th century,
took half breeds and full breeds away
for better education
better discipline
under the arm of religion
under the words of the
clapper-strap happy
brothers & nuns.
This "ideal" infiltration:
assimilation of indigenous minds
institutionalized them to redefine
families without children:
paid out by Indian affairs or church funds,

children without family:
paid out in neglect, abuse, most often moribund.

Take their picture
at Isle a la Crosse, Paddle Prairie, or   Edmonton.
Expose the rules that trapped them into the supposed solution:
No talking to opposite sex
No speaking native tongue
No place for child's play
No thought for imagination
                                        Reveal slow, develop
control.
Thousands died, first year of the process.
Souls swallowed up by child labour
no breath for a savoir
only time enough to pray on Roman Catholic food
malnourishment filled their plates at dinnertime:
blue milk over glue porridge
hard brown bread rapped like knuckles on tabletop.

This is our history, not our neighbours' ride.
People we call "founders" carried out cultural genocide.

Well I say a prediction should have been made,
so we could've been saved
so he could've been saved
from intergenerational distress.
Distrust
that man across from you on the bus is our brother.
His mother, one of the kids from the school.
Her son, a hobbling fool.
Drool is medicine fix now
alcoholic blessing is his prayer
and do we ever ask
How
he came to be this way?

Passed out in front of us
passed off as
"Damn Native, drunken scum,"

driven to a life of sum.
What about the picture behind his slumber?
What about the picture they ripped in the flame?
Sacred flame:
that for many years the only heat that nourished the child.

There's a smudge here.
Somewhere beneath the wild page
sage burns deeper than sores
and these wounds can be healed
if only we take time now.
Don't bow your heads down
Look me in the eye
and may this land mark my words
There's no time like the present
to speak up and
be heard.

Expose it.
Expose THIS.

Shone Abet

Queer Girl

dyke
lesbian
straight girl
woman
bisexual
homosexual
riot girl
butch
femme
in the middle girl
lipstick
chap stick
just call me
Queer Girl

sew a label on my skin
I'll tear it free and let it bleed
poke and prod to fence me in
I'll slip and slide and strip between
the lines will blur
this poet will scream
this fire bellied queer girl
will hurl her knuckles at the sky
all black and blue from years of lies
of who and what and where and when
of generation upon generation
until time and love and light emerge
a gender fucking bender nation
of girls will be boys
and boys will be girls
and any labels worn
will be chosen
not hurled
in innocence direction
not based on genetics
or fear of infection

and if definition
is what you need
define yourself
you can't define me with
dyke
lesbian
straight girl
woman
bisexual
homosexual
riot girl
butch
femme
in the middle girl
sporty
granola
my she's a big girl
maybe you didn't hear me
I said
just call me
Queer Girl

See I've worn all your labels
tried 'em all on for size
but the boundaries they carry
don't suit the size of my expression
I belong to a clan that defies definition
you can't wrap me up
all neat and tidy
tattoo my ear
so later you can find me
I'll define myself
when I feel the need
then strip down naked in order to succeed
I'll shed the labels
like layers of skin
of uptown and downtown and trailer
take this trash out
before it starts to stink of bigotry
before we let it poison the infantry
yeah I'll shed these labels

as fast as you can paste 'em to me
see today I was a boy and
tomorrow I'll be a girl
and the day after that
well who knows for sure, but
try and label my ass again
you might end up with a fat...
stare or glare
and just in case you don't understand
let me drop this request
and make it a demand
let me check my command
of the English language
then break it down
spell it out
stand up here
and shout it out loud for you
I'm all of what came before
and all that's soon to follow...

I'm a...
dyke
lesbian
straight girl
woman
bisexual
homosexual
riot girl
butch
femme
in the middle girl
lipstick
chap stick
urban and suburban girl
uptown
downtown
been around the block girl
but if you need something simpler
just call me
Queer Girl!

Shone Abet

body beautiful

body beautiful
turns my head
opinionated
underrated
made her way
creative
black and white
why fight what this is
or is not
yes she is
body beautiful
super spiritual
doesn't make time for the superficial
and what's the rush
let the hush
fall over the crowd
over the heart
let what this is or is not
start in its own time
savor the flavor of courtship she calls it
novel concept
is this the key
to wait and see
what might unfold
into the Bold and Beautiful
day time
night time
anytime
drama mamma
she is not about smoke and mirrors
but a lost art of truth
hold the vermouth
and spare her the olives
this girl is straight up strong
doesn't give a damn if you think she belongs

and why should she
she is body beautiful

Andrea von Wichert

Stop Doing Reiki on Me!!!!

(a dialogue in 2 voices)

STOP DOING REIKI ON ME!!!!

What!?

You're doing it …

I don't know what –

Don't give me that. You're doing reiki right now, under the table. I can see your hand moving. JUST STOP IT.

Wow, you really WANT to be angry all the time!

This is not about ME – whenever anyone disagrees with you, or suddenly it might seem like you're not actually right all the time, instead of arguing, communicating, oh, admitting you might be wrong: dealing with it, you just fucking start reiki-izing them in secret.

I'm just concerned that all this seething hostility of yours is going to make you sick, geez, try to do some people a favour …

Don't you reiki guys –

– that's reiki MASTERS –

– Reiki MASTERS have some kind of code of ethics or anything on doing distance healing without the person's permission? I went to shaman school, you know the basic class for beginners, and we were told that our spirits HAVE to ask your spirits first before we're supposed to really do anything.

Well, maybe your spirits already told my spirits that you need reiki.

There's no way they'd do that!

How do you know? When was the last time you entered into an altered state of consciousness by using repetitive percussion to change your brain wave patterns from alpha to theta so you can journey into non ordinary reality to consult with spirit guides?

When the cat was missing last winter! Anyway, my relationship to my spirit guides is none of your business. That's it, you control freak, I'm doing an intervention.

A what?

An INTERVENTION – if you can interrupt our argument with some mystical energy disruption, I'm just doing a fucking intervention all over your ass.

You can't do an intervention with just one person.

Who says?

Everybody.

You know what your problem is. You have some blockage in your second chakra that compels you to try to control everyone and everything in your life.

Oh yeah?! Well, your first chakra is so totally fucked up by your tribal misconceptions that you assume anyone who is trying to help you is actually trying to divest you of your personal power!

Is not!

Is so! So you're just leaking energy from your first and third, but oh no, you don't need reiki …

Whatever.

Fine.

Look. I'm sorry. When you do reiki on me without my permission, I feel like my emotional and spiritual bodies are being violated.

Sorry, that was not my intention. When you get angry at me for doing reiki, I feel like my concern for you is being rejected.

Technically, if you're acting in good faith and your shamanic intention is to help, your spirits don't have to ask. And my spirits would be appreciative. I didn't mean to yell at you.

That's ok. I understand that I'm only a mirror and you're just projecting your own self-hatred onto the universe. No biggie. That's where you are right now and I accept that.

Andrea von Wichert

Small Me

Small me was petulant.
So to escape the day
I slept

I did nothing

But in my dreams
I went to the zoo
rode a train forever
walked an alligator
and held the Huge in my arms

Skip Stone

8-bit Villain

I am so hard for you to ignore
I am so much more than some Commodore 64 happy ending high score.
No, I'm a score to settle
I'm that score to beat,
musically I'm a score set to *blips* and *beeps*
I exist mind, body, and console amidst two red buttons, and a **black** cross control.
Atari? Hardly.
But you'll spend every waking minute trying to harm me,
and I just laugh as those minutes turn into hours
'cause, really, I'm the reason you haven't showered.
I am sleepless nights
and a lack of nutrition,
I am everything you despise
you see, that's me,
I'm those bags underneath your eyes.
You look like a wreck 'cause you haven't slept,
this isn't a gym, but you're covered in sweat
and from what?
I mean, you haven't done shit.
All you've done is sit with your eyes glazed over and your mouth open a bit,
my whole existence is about getting you pissed.
You see, I'm that dog from *Duck Hunt* that laughs when you miss
I'm the reason why your thumbs twitch,
why they ache and they itch for just one more hit
like, "Shit! I just gotta beat this bitch, then I can quit. I mean it!"
But naaaaw, I've heard it all. I've seen it.
Oh, you don't believe it?
Then make the sign of the cross to your 8-bit Jesus:
up, up
down, down
left, right, left, right
all day, and all night you pray to me until you've seen the light

which is just the glow from your TV screen,
and right about now your friends are wondering just where the fuck you've been.
"Has he died?"
"No, but to tell you the truth he ain't really alive. He's locked inside, won't come out
and has lost his mind. I went to visit him over the weekend. I put my ear to the door and I
heard him speaking, he was saying,

'C'mon, man, you can beat him!' To himself.
I know this because I only heard him and nobody else."
And that's when I know that I've done my job.
When I've converted you
from just some plain Joe
to some insane slob.
I went from harmless entertainment to brand new game-God.
Who am I?
well, I have so many names
from Gannon to Bowser to even Mother Brain,
it's all the same
I AM DONKEY FUCKING KONG!
I'm everything in the game that tries to do you wrong,
and even when you cheat and you have to use codes
it just lets me know you can't leave me alone.
Until I'm defeated you just have to know how this is gonna go.
You've got to find out for yourself
so you stay locked away in your living room cell
and you can't walk away from your personal hell
From me,
your new reason for living
The **only** thing here that keeps you from winning.
So, c'mon, fight me
'cause I am the almighty
8
bit
villain

Skip Stone

Every 15

I swear to God
I must think of you, like, every 15 minutes,
so in the tabloids of my brain your fame is never finished.
There's just these new issues with all these photos of you.
I've got every single copy
and I don't just leaf through.
You're in my thoughts like paparazzi shots
a steady stream of images of you in random spots.
Relax. I'm not one to stalk,
But since you do live in my mind,
I've been known to circle the block a few times
and when you walk by it's like you're crossing the street from each corner of my eyes.
click. That's you walking.
click. Ha, I love this one, it's of you and me talking.
You see, my favorite photographs are the ones where I'm making you laugh.
I don't know how long this'll last
so could I please get your autograph?
Just make it out to Jon, with love, right there.
Sign one more and I swear I'll get outta your hair.
OK, I'm bluffing, could you please sign a dozen of these photos?
Since I don't know where this is gonna go,
I have no idea where this is headed,
I just wanna prove that, "I knew her once, and I'll never forget it."
Your name stands out in my mind like some giant headline
sometimes combined with mine like
"Donna-than."
I know that ain't clever,
but it's my way of acknowledging that we're actually together.
'Cause through all the gossip and all our friends chattin'
it's actually me who's usually asking,
"How the fuck did this happen?"
But I don't dwell on it too often

'cause I'd rather be with you actually talking, walking, making you laugh
and, of course, when you're not looking, taking mental photographs
that last and last and last.

So while our friends speculate
"Is that her new man?"
just because we've been seen in public possibly holding hands,
it doesn't really matter, 'cause the bottom line is,
and I know this is really hard for you to understand,
I'm amazed that you actually like me
'cause I'm, like,
your number one fan.

White Noise Machine

Heartbreak

You know what I miss?
Heartbreak.
I miss how the angle of shadow that a single branch cuts across sunlight of a summer day contains, for the lost, 40,000 haiku on loneliness.

I miss having an excuse for being slovenly, the kind that elicits sympathetic dialogue from bartenders that makes me feel like I'm in a noir film, rather than "Don't steal the pint glasses." It only happened once!...Twice. I needed a trophy of my fracas with failure, a fragile facsimile of my fallen heart, once so full and frothy and overpriced, now empty and filmed in fingerprints. "Laws? Laws are for the living, and inside I am dead. She has stolen my heart, so I have stolen this...glass."

So, I guess I miss the drama.

And the insight into music! The deep appreciation for chords. Like, E minor, and...well, that's it. But that's everything! All you need is three notes: E, B, and another E.
E is for "everything is pain."
B is for "boobies."
And E is for "everything is pain."

Crushes don't do it for me anymore. I want to be crushed, spindled, folded, mutilated, bent, broken, beaten, bound then thrown in a garbage bag, driven behind the grocery store and tossed in a dumpster like the discarded Finnish porn you don't want your neighbours to know about. Where I could rummage around for bagels and pity fucks from dumpster-diving crusty punks.

Forget crushes, I'm talking heartbreak like influenza. Heartbreak that lays you out for weeks, where everything has this aura of luscious morbidity like a migraine brought to you by Edgar Allan Poe, where crying in your bedroom is like puking in the bathroom, friends knocking on your door, "Dude…are you ok in there?" Heartbreak like strep. Heartbreak like bronchitis. Heartbreak like mono, where you can't move your neck and people bring you fruit.

I'm talking heartbreak directed by Stanislavski, method acting heartbreak, where I "feel my way through it" and "find my major motivation" for every beat.

I want the half-digested detritus of love to bubble in my heart like magic mushrooms in my intestines. When I look at people I don't want to see their faces, but busted open pomegranates or diamonds dipped in molasses and motor oil. I want to bathe in people's secret poetic offal like a only a leper can live with other lepers and find the strength that will live only with weakness, like a bird that sits in the mouth of a crocodile.

So come on. [Mic pound on heart] Don't you just wanna fatten that up and slaughter it? Fill it up like a kettle then put it on to boil?

Gnaw through my ribcage and ask me if you look beautiful with my blood on your chin. Put on a bathing cap and frolic in the arterial spurt like a 1930's dance revue. Kiss me once then break my spine – or, better yet: take your time. Casual lovin's like harsh words in a subway station. Dancefloor dalliances are just a barfight. Kisses out back are like a mugging. I don't wanna be jumped in an alley, I wanna be taken down. I want to be the target of a carefully orchestrated assassination.

Play double agent with my friends. Rig elaborate traps with words, poison your loins and induce me to drink, just make me think, make me work to survive, they should count the bruises to see how long I survived. Steal my secrets and seduce people with them. Smuggle me out in microfiche. Make me clear my name before the House Committee on Unamourous Activities. "This man has done no wrong, and we must get him drunk!"

People should hit their heads on the heartbreak trailing after me. Its particles should refract light. It should open a rift through which the Elder God of Chaos, Cthulu himself, would emerge to console me.

"Here, dude, I brought you the writhing bodies of ten thousand mortal virgins."

"Oh, thanks, Cthulu. But, I'm not hungry."

My heartbreak should change newspaper headlines to poetry as I pass. It should make me work for everything and rely on no one. It should blot out the sun like a nuclear winter, driving all those below to make desperate love and hopeful riots. We're talking heartbreak to pre-empt sitcoms here, to interrupt throne speeches. Heartbreak that stares into the camera and says, "I'm coming for you next, viewing public."

This should be heartbreak I can float out to sea on, and the distant, collapsing star by which I navigate.

Who can do this for me? Before you answer, let me tell you the rest.

What I'm looking for is a monument, like a black hole is to the star it was. Build your empire in me then let it crumble. Make me scramble through sprawl collecting what beauty I can before heading for the outskirts, to return to where I began with what wonders I could salvage. What I am asking of you, as the satellites ask of the asteroids, is to love me.

Approach my borders with the promise of utter destruction, which means you must some day arrive at the core of me and bask in the untold majesty of that which you seek to replace.

To say I miss heartbreak is like saying I miss some city I've never lived in; what I really miss was getting there. The city was just someplace to rest, to eat, to dance out the road stories you couldn't speak. A place to put fuel in the tank before you start moving again, caressing the road, seducing the horizon to stillness.

White Noise Machine

Advertising

You are the most important person in the world
you ugly, fat, scrawny, stupid, nerdy, terrified little stink monkey
We know your continued success is crucial to you
you fake
you fraud
you scribbling little failure
And we know the safety of your loved ones
is your ever-continuing priority
you pissant

you're gonna die you're gonna die you're gonna die you're gonna die
you're gonna die you're gonna die you're gonna die you're gonna die
you're gonna die you're gonna die you're gonna die you're gonna die
you're gonna die you're gonna die you're gonna die you're gonna die
you're gonna die you're NEVER gonna die! as long as you've got fresh breath.

YES, FRIENDS, EVERYTHING DEPENDS ON YOU!
It is smoggy because you smell bad
A polar bear
just killed itself in despair
when we told it
you don't have a laptop
Kim Jong-il vibrates with rage at your woefully untended split ends
Wilderness flees from the controlled fall of our sprawling house like a spurned lover,
secretly hoping that you will chase decisively after it
in a brand-new
SUV

Boobies boobies boobies boobies boobies boobies boobies boobies
boobies boobies boobies boobies boobies boobies boobies boobies
boobies boobies boobies boobies boobies boobies boobies boobies
boobies boobies
bum

Everything is fine! Something is missing.
And it'll last forever – so don't delay!
Be the first on your block to own your block!
Be the first caller through and receive a personalized recording of
the first caller through;
and be sure to Get It All on Film.

...Did we say film? We meant digital.
Did we say digital? We meant "Network-Ready."
Did we say Network-Ready? We meant Network-*Al*ready.
It's already in the system. We know what you did today before
you've even done it,
and if you don't take a look, you'll have no idea how you're going
to do it.
Your boss sure will appreciate it.

Did you say you hate your job?
Sure you hate your job, everyone hates your job. Your job hates
your job.
And, boy, have we got the answer for you!
And, boy, it's expensive,
so get to work!

Workers, make the boss rich or he won't be able to pay you!
Voters, if you don't vote for someone, who will tell you who to vote
for?
Malcontents, if you don't take advantage of assholes like us, who
will tell the world about assholes like us?
Men, women hate you.
Women, men hate you.
Fags, trannies and dykes

...we don't know how to make money off of you yet.
But we're working on it!

Parents, lie to your kids –
before someone else does.

Kids...your parents are lying to you.

But not us; we care.
Of course we care –
we want your money.
And *you're* the *only one* with *your* money.
Just think of the power!

you pissant.

L.E.V.I.A.T.H.A.N.

Cars

I need you all to listen and **Ford Focus** one what I'm gonna tell you.
Things that we drive reveal a historical tale,
and in some way subconsciously drive us.
You don't need Dodge **Neon** headlights to see that way before
Grand Marquis the **Buick Regals Crown Victoria** that they were on
  a **Nissan Quest**
cuz Prince Henry the **Navigators,**
and other **Plymouth Voyageurs, Ford Explorers**
went on **Expeditions** to **X-Terra** X(Unknown), Terra (Earth or land).
They **Venture** in these **Odysseys** in search of riches,
and upon making their **Discovery**
these **Trail Blazers** were clearly out of their **Honda Element.**
They had various **Buick Rendezvous** with the native Indians.
They had very strange **Honda Accents.**
These people were proud, yet humble.
Intrepid, they handled the bow and arrow with pinpoint **Acura-cy,**
it was insane.
Gracious People of **Integra-ty** and **Legends** of the plains
independent and were **Hyundai Excel**-lent farmers.
People like **Brougham Cadillac De Ville, Le Mans, Pinto**
weren't feeling their **Pontiac Vibe,**
and realized that they weren't getting what they wanted
damn it, these people are just not convertible!
So the **Entourage** returned back to their **Dodge Caravans.**
MacLaren and Mercedes had the **Formula**
One night before the onslaught these persona non gratas
would get piss-drunk listen to **Hyundai Sonatas**
then later **Ford Probe** the situation and
instead of attacking and having an **Armada** at **9(2)9,**
they would ambitiously ambush the Indians at around
Mazda 6(2)6 in the morning using **Sunfire** to burn
the Ottawa Chief **Pontiac**'s teepees and wigwams.
With no qualms.
Killed off the men.

They enjoyed the spoils of war, it was in their nature, they had to have it.
These **Chrysler Prowlers** like **Jaguars** ravaged the poor Indian women
and raped them like **VW Rabbits.**
How the hell could you have a **Honda Accord**
using their gonorrhea, syphilis, smallpox, bubonic plague-infested hands to feel their **Ford Contours.**
That's the **Midas Touch!**
Thanksgiving wasn't about the food that looks great on your plate.
It was a feast to celebrate those they killed and women they raped.
And Custer was a fool for not making his **Pontiac Grand Am-erican Ford Escape.**
Masta, um, I mean **Mazda Protege's** had to **Nissan Maxima**-ize their time
and be **Suzuki Swift**
cuz it was a **Honda Civic** duty to civilize us and all that other Razamatazz.
Mamma Afriqa killing yoazz for gold, diamonds, platinum, emeralds rubies
and even **Mercury Topaz.**
This ain't no fable like Anne of Green Gables,
something smells of skunk like **Mercury Sable.**
In Rwanda we had Huttus chopping down Tutsis like trees with **Cutlass Supremes**
final resting places on the **GMC Safari, Savanah,** and the **Sierra/Cierra**
I asked you: If you listen, then **Ford Focus.**
You might be able to hear the echoes of chants,
the beating of the drums and the throat singers and **Hummers** worshipping the Moon
and performing ceremonial **Sundance.**
In the future they were glimpsing **Le Barons** on **Mustangs** galloping like **Impalas** chasing after two African-American Indians in a white **Ford Bronco**
Yes I'm talking about O.J. Simpson,
Get the hell outta **Dodge, Pickup** what you can
only natives Red **Grand Cherokees** and Black **Nissan Muranos** and **Mulattoes**
have no nationality or land claims according to international laws.

Whether it be the **Chevy Equinox** or **Honda Solstice**
any season is hunting season.
You heard of the **Pathfinder** and **Landrover,** the **Subaru Forrester** known as
Jimmy the **Ranger,**
pulls out his **Beretta** and **Le Sabre** whenever there's danger
hangs out with **Isuzu Troopers,** beats up on kids, think they're built **Ford Tough**
rough and stuff with the afropuff
and then quietly **Ford Escort** you round the corner take you to the
Subaru Outback and give you a tune-up.
How many times we gotta get kicked in the grill or tail pipe?
Get your head **Dodge Ram**'med on the concrete.
Then when you complain about being jacked up you get told that
"THESE ARE THE BRAKES"
totalled from bumper to bumper, feels like you got run over by an 18-wheeller
Uh Oh, better get Maaco!
Lucky they didn't blow your brains out and leave your thoughts on the dashboard
Exhaust fumes is making your **Vision** cloudy
We're being taken for a ride and I'm **Audi.**
But…I'm **Mazda Optimistic** that I jump started a sparkplug or two
to get some of you **Oldsmobile Intrigue**'d.
How long is it going to take for the rest of you to plug into the **Toyota Matrix?**
A **Buick Century?**
Mazda Millenia?
Saturn Eons or…
an **Infiniti?!**

L.E.V.I.A.T.H.A.N.

Survival H_20

Water is the global symbol for purity,
without it we face imminent fatality.
I see the day cometh when we will have none and will all die nasty.
If you haven't noticed
I've got water on the brain like I was hydrocephalic, see?

As we become more cosmopolitan,
and our population increases
we are gradually getting away from the very substance that gives us life.
Every time we dispose of something that's not supposed to be drained or flushed,
we contribute to the destruction of our most valuable resource for vitality,
tragically,
and it's a travesty that technologically we are advanced more so now
than at any other time period,
with the exception of the days of Alkebu-lan (ancient Africa),
but we have plummeted in respect to our decline in morality,
to levels that are abysmal
and it is a dismal shame this is the stark reality.

Never mind that even with hydra-wear contact lenses
we would still be watercolour blind,
hence why I'm not surprised to find that with so much of this stuff on tap
that is this topic has never been tapped nor touched like a virgin.
From don't throw out the baby with the bath water
to desperate house guys turning on the water works
begging, spending money like water splurging
spouting words that flood her mind with H^20 fluidity like
"girl I love you so much, I'll drink your bath water."
If that's your thing
then all hydroelectric power to you!

While writing these lines
my eyes cried ammonia water for certain for you,
cuz soon, we'll be raising the topic of why the tropics is like the Arctic
and the Antarctic is like the tropics
global warming turning into global cooling,
and the driest most barren deserts turn into land o' lakes
just overflowing from pooling.
We all know about cloud formations due to water evaporation
and rainfall due to over-saturation,
which causes condensation,
the vicious cycle begins with our over-consumption,
lack of conservation,
damaging the ecosystem that will leave us like fish out of fresh water,
flip flop till deceased
rapidly growing areas where stagnant waters are cesspools
for new breeds of micro-organisms that cause disease.
Amazing how you can get pneumonia in the form of Legionnaires disease
from "treated filtered" bottled water.
I'm surprised that partygoers popping ecstasy aren't
championing the importance of bottled water,
from what I hear it's all the rage at all the raves.
We graze on it like cows to the slaughter
down to and thru our water
shitstems of filtration.
A lady from Greenpeace who was venting her frustration
told me that due to excessive deforestation,
we're wiping our asses with 5,000 year old trees.
And I jokingly said "all to acquire puffs tissues with soreless soft guarantee."
She didn't find that funny,
she angrily replied, "Mr. running man! You can guarantee that one day you'll be runnin' from the hail, snow, prevailing winds, torrents, freezing rain,
tornadoes, tsunamis a.k.a. tidal waves, other side of the world hurricanes
which will lead to floods, widespread famine,
because come hell or high water we're all gonna pay.

There is no way to escape the wrath.
66 per cent of each and every one of us is made of it,
we're all skating on thin ice, mister
we drink, swim, ski, and bathe with it,
but when Mother Nature gets pissed off we're gunna be afraid of it.
Scientists call it the most vital compound on this planet and the
universal solvent,
you'd think that with all this money going to into it
why does the shituation get compounded
damnit and nothing solved yet.
I call H20 the breast milk of Mother Nature,
that with the nature our sickness we have somehow denatured
all the freaky weather,
that's her way of saying I hate ya.
Hate the fact that industrial to domestic cleansers like
Sani-flush, 2000 Flushes to those scrubbable flushable brushes
gets dumped back into our water supply,
is lining and corroding our pipes can't be gotten rid of.
It's like trying to get all the toothpaste out of the tube,
unless you cut it open to scoop it out,
you can't do it.

Which leads to why they won't tell you about the sludge effect
and how it would cripple the city if they tried to remove it
and how they have to use giant boilers and rubber scrubbers by
separating
the solids from the semi solids
and the semi solids from the not-so-clear-liquids
and the not-so-clear liquids from the clear liquids
and the clear liquids from the "treated" clear liquids
and the "treated" clear liquids from the tested approved chemically
"treated" clear liquids
and the tested approved chemically "treated" clear liquids
from the primary, secondary, quality controlled, tested approved,
specially filtered, chemically "treated," crystal clear liquids
which in actuality is really chlorine and fluoride soup,
which they have the nerve to call water, a.k.a. government juice,
that despite this protest,
I have to consume to stay hydrated to recite this protest.
Now that's thirsty work,

WHEEEW…
I need a drink!

Amanda Hiebert

Linda

She works the mid shift at the Skyline Diner.
Black coffee and bread pudding,
two blocks east of Lansdowne where the action is

Stands five foot two at a hundred and not much more
blondish hair sifted through an elastic band
doesn't wear make-up
eyes so plain you could forget them
I don't want to.

Old lady Helen comes in at four every day.
They talk about Avon and leave-in conditioner
while time punches her $6.40 an hour away.
Joe stumbles in all Jim Beamed up,
orders another with a Blue to chase 'er down to the races,
she shrugs.
At least he's happy.

If I remember correctly, her name is Linda.
My time spent at the Skyline is a popcorn string of hangovers
I'm building up for next Christmas.

She serves me my usual close to eight days a week after hard days' nights
occasionally being joined by heartbroken friends, mediocre lovers
or poets who have come to adopt my couch for the night.
Every now and then she meets someone who's been all of the above,
but that's another story.

She's all of twenty three
but we are her children here…
Joe the drunk, Helen all lipstick and fake nails,
and me: a gypsy who feels tied to a rock,

staring at the scum sheeted across her coffee, looking for the faces
in it.
I'm not depressed
just a little off kilter,
and this is where such people come to congregate,
where the waitress smiles like Mondays don't exist on a calendar.

I want to pretzel my fingers around her ceramic hands,
tell her that the manicures she gives herself every night after eight
don't go unnoticed,
want to ask her how school's going.
But she's got a good seven orders of:
easy-over, sausage, brown-no white, bacon crispy soft poached,
could I have more coffee and a chocolate milk for the little one
please?
scuttling about in her head.
I don't want to be another regular who padlocks her into trite
conversation,
thinking that we're friends.
That's the difference between me and her.
She's here to pay the rent.
But to me,
this booth feels like home.
All burgundy leather lined against wood the colour of cherry-
stained teeth
where it's okay to be a bit of a shipwreck.

See, not so long ago, she noticed my heart breaking,
deconstructing itself into sails the size of thumbnails slipping
through eyelids.
With my sixth refill that day,
a small stack of napkins pressed into the table like an offering:
Dear Linda,
You saved my life. Thank you.

My friend Brendan once joined me.
All ink and paper and omelettes.
Told me he could fall in love with her.
Looked at her with a yellow balloon grin.
I was grateful. Because I want her to be happy.

Some say they left their hearts in San Francisco.
But when I leave this place,
mine will be just two blocks east of Lansdowne where the action is,
in the well-manicured hands of a waitress
named Linda.

Amanda Hiebert

Farm Grandma

She reminds me of the chokecherry trees
knuckles baking under mid July tenacity
Straw hats   mosquito coils
Oh, the things we'll do for pie!

Been hard of hearing since her last Remax convention   late
seventies
That afternoon   the only thing she bid for was more time
to read the lips of the numbers being read

That was the year she retired into 'Mennonite Housekeeping'
raised her children right on borscht   and common sense

The year she learned the art of fluster
stammering and shaky fingered as she   missed the underground
rumble
of her husband's bellow

Good Wives know how to listen   but what if they can't?

My grandfather's words   hundreds of miniature wooden
blocks sliding down crooked floors. His voice, the microwave and
the time all come into the same metronome.

So she's gotta   turn the hearing aid up
Turn the hearing aid up
TURN THE HEARING AID UP
To hear the voices of her grandchildren when they tell her they love
her.

She has   mastered the art   of fluster
And when the aged newspaper tears drip down her cheeks
we write love letters in the crow's nests that our parents built

At seventy seven she asks her dementia-ridden husband to speak up speak up speak up
when he tells her he's leaving
Leaving you. Leaving you. Leaving you.
Opens her wallet. Looking for crisp bills to purchase the time necessary in finding
the sounds of reason in a world gone silent as the church bells ring.

My grandfather sings to the tongue of crazy
while his wife reads her 'Daily Bread' under a magnifying glass
threading the pages with fingers whose nerves have forgotten how to stand still.
THIS is the sight of a fall from grace.
Losing pieces of oneself vowels dripping
From the very word vowel.
A couple sits over dry toast and burnt coffee.
Having built their lives in the hymnals of church pews
The songs are falling the songs are falling the songs are falling out
Soon their will be only prayer and weathered bibles

This afternoon, he will pack his bags for the ninth time this week.
She will see but not hear him curse a marriage he does not remember

Amidst Arthur's after-dinner nap complaints
his wife will count and place his pills
little orange tablets in little orange containers
wash dry fold two loads of laundry
walk the dog
weed the marigolds
check the mail
pluck an ice cream bucket of chokecherries from
the untidy fingernails of their homestead
oh the things we'll do for pie!

All the while praising the Lord in mid July tenacity.
I only wish I could unplug the clouds in my grandmother's ears
so she could finally sing her favorite hymn in key.

Valentino Assenza

Let Me

Let me knock
on your door,
I promise,
it won't be loud
and annoying,
and I promise
it won't be forever,
if you don't open
I'll walk away,
with my hands
in my pockets,
and my head down.

But if you open
the door,
and let me in,
I promise
I won't have
any ulterior motives,
I just want
to talk to you,
let me take my coat off
and sit down,
and let me hear you
offer me a drink,
and whether it's citrus,
or alcoholic,
let me enjoy it just
as much,
'cause it came from your hands.

Let me let you know
that the day
has brought me to my knees,
and let me show you

what it feels like
when life is no longer
my ally,
let me bury my face
in you,
'cause the air is too thick
and I need you
to smother me
some relief.

Let me look into your eyes,
and let me get lost
in your mystical maze,
and let's have
that simultaneous
silent prayer between us
before we kiss,
and when you finally let
me put my lips to yours,
let's both be experts
at not letting go,
let me put my hands on you,
and let me feel
your hands on me.

Let me take you
to the bedroom
by the hand,
and let me undress you,
let me hear you
remind me
that I just wanted to talk,
and I'll tell you I did,
'cause when I
take off your panties,
I'll say hi to her,
and when I take off your bra
I'll say hi to her and her,
and when you let me
lay you on the bed

and you let me know
that you're ready
to have this dialogue
with me,
I promise
I'll be detailed,
eloquent,
and articulate,
I promise to live up to
my words,
and evoke your ecstasy,
I'll speak to you
in tongues,
but you'll understand it all,
and respond
in your own goddess speak,
and any thing we don't say
we'll let the sheets,
bedposts,
gibberish, and moans,
fill it all in.

Let me lie next to you,
in a comatose frenzy,
with the alarm clock
reading 4:42 a.m.,
the sun cradled in
night's arms ready
spring for the morning,
let's let bliss
cradle us,
'cause we're the
unsung heroes
in our own dream worlds.

And when the sun comes up
and you're sitting on a chair
in front of me,
and you ask me
what I wanted to talk about,

let me tell you
that somehow coffee tastes richer
this morning,
how the world is
spinning at just the right speed,
that making you smile
makes it all worthwhile,
that when we're spinning
around in circles,
and out of control,
sometimes it's all
a part of it,
and in a haze like this,
I'd rather see you than nothing.

Let's go for that walk,
it's mild out,
let's go down that path
with all the twist and turns,
and trees,
and bridges,
and streams,
I don't know how far
we'll get,
the wind might blow
in our face,
and the rain might fall
hard,
but sooner or later
the sun'll come out.

Valentino Assenza

One Saved Message

There are many barometers
that I will use
to measure how well
or poorly
my life is going:

how much money I have,
what the scale says
in the morning,
going into work
and finding out
I'm still not fired.

But lately,
there is one thing
that speaks to me
even louder
than all of these things.

It's how many messages,
I have on my voicemail.
No…
that's wrong,
it's the way
in which I'm told
how many messages
are on my voicemail.

Lately,
the Call Answer Lady,
has been telling me:

"You have
one saved message."

Sometimes,
she'll be a little more
enthusiastic saying:

"You have
one new message!"

And very rarely,
she'll get excited saying:

"You have
two new messages!"

But lately,
it's been nothing but
the unenthusiastic:

"You have,
one saved message."

And why, I often wonder,
does she stop there?
Why doesn't she say:

"You have one saved message.
You pathetic fuck,
the word loser
doesn't even begin
to scratch the surface when
it comes to you,
why don't you just do
the world a favour
and crawl back
into your hole.

"You have one saved message,
'cause you jerk off
to anything,
whether it's select scenes
of Salma Hayek in

From Dusk 'Til Dawn,
or Phoebe Cates in
Fast Times at Ridgemont High
or that shitty soft porn
on CityTV late on Friday night.

"And if there's no porn around
hell,
you'll pick up the box of pancake mix
and jerk off
to Aunt Jemima.
You have one saved message,
because thanks to all those
years of burgers, pizza,
and beer,
you haven't seen your
dick in over a decade.
Who knows,
it might have
more messages than you.

"You have one saved message,
'cause your last ten dates
have ended with,
'Can we be friends?'
And sometimes
You're stupid enough to
say yes.
And you'll fall in love
with anyone,
a girl smiles at you
on the street
and all of a sudden,
you're picturing the wedding,
the dinner parties,
Freedom 55,
the summer house.

"You have one saved message,
'cause when you're in the car

by yourself,
you'll actually sing along
to 'Never Surrender' by Corey Hart,
cause you really did
give a shit
when Dylan McKay broke up
with Brenda Walsh,
'cause when you're flipping
around the channels,
and you end up in the
middle of a Golden Girls episode,
you'll actually watch it to the end,
and 'cause you still cry,
at the end of the movie,
when Kevin Costner's character
asks his Dad,
if 'he wants to have a catch'."

…it's true

And this in essence
could very well
bring me down,
it could end me.
The Call Answer lady
makes a strong case,
but she gives me an out,
and all I need
is to have the balls
to take it…

"To erase this message,
press seven
to save it,
press nine…"

Hmmm.......

Kevin Matthews

The Love Song of Roy G. Biv

when first we made love
red
enflamed arteries dilate in raunchy primates
pupils engorged like dinner-plates
to take in all this red
rusty red lantern, fire engine candy
ripe red raspberry, rash and randy
red like sunsets underwater
we didn't think it could get any hotter

until we made love orange
orange like fires in forges for steel
blazing building blinding orange – people running out
but orange love makers run into inferno
to the citrus heart so juicy and tart
flamethrower fresh squeezed appetite for orange nothing can curb it
but maybe the taste of a sweet orange sherbet

so when we made yellow love
glowing hello lemon jello l - o - v - e
sun bursts nova behind eyelids shut tight tingling
yellow like syrup down spinal synapses
syncopated honey and sunshine dust in a goldmine
I drew a line
I drew a line for you, o what a thing to do
and then again we made love new

made it green
in dark nooks of rainforests safe and unseen
lily lips, rosehips and venus flytraps
ever green while insect life cycles elapse
and green for vital, green for go
slowly though we grow
grass blades burst through concrete blocks
strong and sure as bamboo stalks

fresh as dew on you and me waking on the lawn
love made green goes ever on

into blue
we made love blue! made it true
blue nude superheroes soaring through
skies or oceans deep and still
or cool and thin from mountain stream
blue crèpe kites flying through limitless space we thought would
  never end until

we made love indigo.
O, in we go
painfully slow and just so – in dig o
jazz licks, drumsticks, body be-bop softshoe tricks
collarbone solo, vibrato lips
kisses riff down epidermis thermal hermeneutics
fingering fretboard up and down neck
had to take five like Brubeck
so sing low, sing low and let me know
are you with me indigo
only one more hue to go:

violet love
long-wave radiating resonating
echoes back, reward for waiting
no n in this ultraviolet
pilot me through foggy sea of violet
va va voom
rising up to fill the room with azalea also honeysuckle, lavender,
  bluebell
bubble and tumble through a purple sea with me
lost in violet love of measureless degree

and that's about all that can be said
until again we make love red

Kevin Matthews

Give it 2 me

i'm taking on the break of dawn with sinister devices
i'm taking a class on forecasting stock prices
i'm taking down names of the naughties and nices
i'm taking particular note of the names appearing twice

i'm taking up knitting – and spitting
and splitting by stealth; i'm taking stock of everyone else's wealth
i'm taking over – doses – of chocolate and sunshine

i'm taking up space and time
demanding your attention, spanning the room
withstanding your staring, detachment and gloom
HEAR ME SAY: BOOM! i'm taking that silence with me to the tomb.

i'm taking Prozac with peas
i'm taking leaks against trees
i'm taking chances with phonetically transmitted diseases
i'm taking teenaged girls – on shopping sprees
i'm taking pictures at the reception and the pickles and the cream
  cheese
extra cream cheese, and i'm not saying please.

i'm taking the bus to the rodeo
snowblower floor show ropin and ridin and blowin some dough
taking wooden nickels and Snickers bars from cowboy clowns in
  tiny cars
i'm taking a rocket to sirius – the dog star
yes i take it seriously – maybe too far.

So i'm taking it easy
i'm taking deep breaths and counting to nine
i'm taking the railcart down into the abandoned mine
i'm making time for cheaper wine
i'm taking the steeper – but shorter – incline.

i'm taking out competition like silverfish in the kitchen
i'm taking candy from babies & steaks from alligators – i'm taking
more to save for later.

i'm taking another deep breath and counting to seven
i'm taking the peaceable parkway to heaven
i'm taking one more shot at failure, & then i'm giving up
i'm taking two more sips from this cappuccino cup
one to cool me down, another to pick me up.
i'm taking that action, i'll raise you a fraction
taking orders and french fries from customers' plates
taking care of fragile freights for reasonable commission rates
i'm taking your money and making you wait
i'm taking the heat in the captain's seat
taking my lumps from the press and provoking debate
i'll take on the state!

i'm taking this exit before it's too late.

A. Gregory Frankson, a.k.a. Ritallin

Drum

Distinguish the drum you hold between your knees from the one you hold within your chest

Decipher the message from God above when rhythms infect you at His urgent behest

The beat of life that throbs like sexual energy preparing to share its promise of a genesis of life

Pollinates the ecology of my tortured psychology causing seismology to dislodge my torment and dormant strife

Can you recite all night the stories of glory that define the strength of your roots from the core of the earth

If not, don't sweat those who can and I demand you learn the lessons necessary for personal cultural rebirth

I cannot claim to be a fount of knowledge unless I fill my well with the life's blood of my history

And conduct my life, through my actions, values and morality with the requisite level of consistency

Because I cannot be a righteous human when my mind, body and soul are simultaneously at fundamental odds

The key to joy within your life can be found in synchronicity of your existence that sacrifices your vanity to the gods

Because once I realized I wasn't living right, the decision to change my ways was the easiest first step

And now that I've set that foot forward there are so many more that I must take before I draw my last breath

Setting forth on this mission is a shock to the part of me content with my flaws and frailties equipping me to function daily

But it's hard to be content when guilt and remorse and a desire for better living assail me

So I stride confident in the belief I can achieve all I can as Garvey once taught a dark race

And with one hand on my drum and the other on my heart I steal forward step by step to claim my space

Beautiful is the place of glory being held for me by the ancestors who lived lives designed to seal my fate

And Providence shows me unbelievers will bow low before the blessed who move from last to first in their mental state

Distinguish the drum you hold between your knees from the one you hold within your chest

And beat the skins for liberty, love and hope claimed on this battlefield of life – my history demands nothing less.

A. Gregory Frankson, a.k.a. Ritallin

Feel the Old School

So come on now everybody
Everybody clap your hands
Because this poem that I'm dropping
Straight into your dome
Gon' bring back the old school jams

Check it out!

Keep on walkin' till you feel the real love
Like Luther gave to us before he left for up above
They reminiscence over you and that's true
Cuz love is a wonderful thing, ain't mad at you
But Chuck D. and Flava Flav are in another summer
They down with the king when they hear the funky drummer
And watching fast feet of Rick James the super freak
Givin' lots of TLC to ladies – so I creep
Backstage to get blazed, you know what's up
I'm a blunt gettin' smoked and I can't wake up
KRS and LONS, Nice n' Smooth and Cypress Hill
They fill me with my hip-hop hooray with mad skill
Don't beat it when you're bad, it's dangerous and off the wall
This thriller's like the lady in my life after all
So don't fall, take it slow cuz you got nothing to fear
Especially with New York – ya out there?

So come on, people come on
That's right
So come on, come on, now people come on
That's it

Mr. Dobolina, Mr. Bob Dobolina
He was chillin' with the Hammer when he asked him "have you
  seen her?"
And Missy Misdemeanor, leaning on her Beamer
Was looking for her keys so she could go sim simma

But RZA and GZA fo' shizza were with a
Whole group of niggas who were tryin' to get bigga
But Biggie, Biggie, Biggie can't you see
That ODB was living in Mariah's fantasy
Then Mary J. B., like Talib to get by
Was chilling with the Method Man, that ain't no lie
She pulled a switch like Will, commercial mov-ah
Hitting people with the 411 like Grand Puba
And the tribe was on a quest while on award tour
Cuz you, you got what I need and even more
This music is a passion, it fashioned my soul
Merged the new with old and left me like Janet – in control

Throw your hands in the air
And wave 'em like you just don't care
So all the people in the room
That feel the old school
Let me hear you bawl out oh yeah
(oh yeah)
Oh yeah!
(oh yeah)
Scream!
(ahhhhh!)

So come on now everybody
Everybody clap your hands
Because this poem that I'm dropping
Straight into your dome
Gon' bring back the old school jams
Check it out!

Kaie Kellough

vox versus

I was there.
– Walt Whitman

i.

you can't say
to blacks today:

"if history were real estate
you wouldn't own one
stolen canadian acre."

we who slaved with the panis
bit frost in preston
broke and seeded frozen scotian ground

you can't say
to blacks today: "the nation's heart
don't be or bop beneath your sternum." we

seamed by faults: the coquihalla, the 401
who feel a nation's muscled pulse
in black asphalt, a canadiana suite
a diasporan iration

can't be cautioned: "be
have or be deported." whose caustic
grandfathers portered? whose maroon
ancestors,
xpelled from xamaica's blue mountains
to scova notia, were spelled back
back back
to ac-
ir-
far

back back back
to the black
man
lan'?

you can't blame
blacks today: "you sow violence and woe
in t-dot-o"

smith & wesson ain't head
quartered on vaughn & oak

wood, no.
the metro po-po ain't
no *kardinal official* in blue you

can't castigate
blacks today
when pale prairie

studs get mailed
back from iraq in black
caskets wrapped in flags

and newsprint flak. you can't balk
when peckerwoods endear
one another as nigger, headphones

married to the boom-bap, seeding rap
in both errs –

or when cornrows kink
your daughters' heirs

we are, have been, will be –

hear

ii.

with hexes for eyes
i stare through history
achoo. ghosts
hover between our gazes:

residential schools
slavers' fields. the lash
blinks; these visions
blip to priceville, preston
rickety log-cabins
windows blinded by jaundiced
news that notes no
slouch-hatted black
pioneer, royal blue
liveried porter, conk-headed
ivory-tickler, black cassock'd
united church minister.
these ghosts shift

to black glyps, black sparks, black stars, stretch legs
and crawl, spiders, shimmer
into silver

webs, refract
in your face, facts.

Kaie Kellough

one fine mass morn

for my wife, kim

when brass sun bops bright on the horizon
and dawn-birds' free-jazz jangles my dream
i'll rise and claim the new day, my fine, hard-won prize

i'll saunter to the stream and stretch by its banks
laugh with the fish-flash in the ripples, bow to the trees and hills
breathe the breeze that blazes all that's green

then pack my leavin' trunk, cast away my troubles
blow a kiss goodbye, a butterfly, to my sweet florence town
gear up my old pickup, hum a blues to the engine's rattle

rickety-ride to the forty-ninth, lay down my paid-for papers
cross on into canaan land, and though i'll weep
for babylon, for the statue of sojourner truth, bronze abolitionist,
  my spark, my sister spirit

i'll learn to love marie-joseph-angelique, incendiary architect of
  montreal's steel and concrete
its spray-paint spit on brick, its unfree city schtick –
i'll seek

massachusetts birches in my baby's long-armed embrace
i'll sway as he holds me, swings me, sing as he thrills me
hear the stream and the dawn-birds in his hot words

lay down to sleep by his side, when the moon rears
its bleached cranium in the sky, close my eyes and dream
my loneliness is dust, is done. a new day is won

Ardath Whynacht

Sliding

In your last moments you think about a lot of things.
But it all happens so fast it's a wonder you can think of any one
thing at all.

They say that time stops when you start to fall,
and you can see the whole world beneath you, so clear and profound
as you float higher and higher up into the clouds…

There are those people who have been there and somehow returned;
speaking prose of that eternal night,
descending within the tunnel of light,
a light that shines so bright but doesn't burn
and they speak of how much it changes you.

Sometimes you can't hold it and you shit yourself
and it's messy and ugly as you slowly sputter and fade away.

You can think about the things that you've done wrong
but it's pointless because in seconds you are just…
Gone.

And it doesn't matter anymore.

For much of my life I expected that in those moments
– hurtling toward oblivion –
I would come to some *profound* realization:
something transformative, informative and holy!

I have thought of countless different scenarios for what I would
find on the other side.

Even science backs up the theory of life after death,
as the Law of Transfer of Energy states:
energy cannot be created or destroyed – just transferred into another form

I am a pretty energetic person,
so I've always wondered where I would go and what I would
become.

Maybe we all become constellations in other galaxies
and other beings much like us will look way up high
and birth legends to explain our existence in their sky.

But…

Doing 80 on a curve I've ridden hundreds of times,
when I felt my rear wheel sliding and I knew I had to choose
between a guardrail with a 15-foot drop to the ocean and rocks,

or

the slippery shoulder,

I don't remember anything after that but

Sliding.

Sliding into nowhere
and that was it.

And, when he told me he saw me and my bike slipping and then
flipping end-over-end into the creek

I thought he was *shitting* me.

Because I only remember being nowhere.

And despite the mud up to my knees
I still didn't believe him until I saw the damage.

With no precaution for spinal or head injuries I leapt from nowhere
to the remains of my bike and I wailed.

But it still didn't register.
Incredulous stares still didn't clue me in
to the obvious:
I'd ridden headfirst into death and walked away.

But I had no awareness of this fact,
I was more just pissed that my tail fairing had snapped
and I only grimaced when a passing car ran over the remains of my mirror.

And when he told me a friend of his with a similar ride snapped his spine on a guardrail and died just two weeks earlier –
I just laughed.

I laughed. And there was silence.

It took me a few days to figure out why they were all so upset.

Why my father clutched his chest and the cop just scratched his head…

I walked on with no memories except for the moment of nowhere
between when I chose to live or chose to be dead
when I surrendered to the shoulder.

They all agreed it was a miracle.

But, I don't feel lucky.

I almost wish that I'd snapped a bone or twisted something down
in the creek, and come up wincing and bloody
because at least I would have felt something.

Now I don't know what I'm supposed to look forward to.

I can't decide if I experienced nothing profound because it just
wasn't my time
Or, because there really is nothing on that other side.

So I'm scared.
I'm not scared of the crash or the snapping of spines.

But I'm scared
that there'll be nothing there waiting for me the next time

I start to slide.

Ardath Whynacht

Love song for the audience

I bring words mouth to mouth
And the space between us stretches taut like a guitar string

But please,
Ignore these words

I want to make the silence sing

I don't want you hear them,
I want you to
Taste them
Place them
Delicately on the centre of your tongue
Until each word dissolves into the pockets around your gums
And then swallow

(I long to speak my words deep into the space where you're hollow)

Listen for the pauses
It's in those moments you can glimpse the merry dance
of the skeletons in my closet

Dancing a maritime jig and giving the finger

– I apologize for their lewd behaviour –

I can't control them
I suppose what makes me a *poet*
(An inability to speak to those I love)
With an irrepressible need to run to a stage or a page to express those
Inexpressible and inappropriate moments

Maybe this whole spoken ritual is just about uncovering secrets.

...Trudging up to the stage to lift your skirt so that all can see *this:*

We are not so different.

Editor Bio

David Silverberg has been involved in Canada's spoken word community since 2001. He founded the now-defunct Suburban Spoken Word in North York, Ontario, and then created Toronto Poetry Slam, where he currently serves as host and artistic director. He has also curated spoken word programming at Word on the Street, the Luminato Festival of Arts & Creativity, the Brampton Indie Arts Festival, the Words Aloud Festival in Durham, Ont., the Wavelength music series, and many more. David is one of two Toronto committee chairs on the board for the annual Canadian Festival of Spoken Word. He is part of the Toronto poetry troupe Last Call Poets, and his most recent book of poetry is *Bags of Wires* (LyricalMyrical). He is managing editor of DigitalJournal.com, a citizen journalism website. *Mic Check* is his first (and hopefully not last) anthology of spoken word he has been asked to edit. Find him at www.torontopoetryslam.com.

Contributor Bios

Shone Abet is counted as one of Canada's most OUTspoken word activists. Engaging audience members through conversation and suggestion, Abet reflects on personal identity, experience, body image, activism and popular culture. Her performance credits include: the Calgary International Spoken Word Festival, Canadian Festival of Spoken Word, Eve Ensler's *The Vagina Monologues*, and One Yellow Rabbit's High Performance Rodeo.

Barbara Adler was the youngest performer to win a spot on the acclaimed Vancouver Poetry Slam team, at the age of 18. Now a four-time member, Barbara has continued performing to become one of Vancouver's best known full-time poets. Performance highlights include The Winnipeg International Writers Festival (2004), The Vancouver International Folk Festival (2004, 2006, 2007), The Vancouver International Readers and Writers Festival (2007), three International Fringe Theatre Festivals, and the two CBC Poetry Face-Off Contests. Barbara has toured internationally both with the spoken word-music band, The Fugitives, and as a solo spoken word artist.

Valentino Assenza has been a published poet and known spoken word artist for the last decade in and around the Toronto area. He has performed his poetry in several of the major Toronto venues, and has also performed in other parts of Canada such as Vancouver, and Montreal. He has published three chapbooks of poetry, belongs to a spoken word collective called Last Call Poets, and runs his own spoken word poetry series, Cryptic Chatter. He can be contacted via his web page at http://valentino.coffeehouse.ca.

Moe Clark a.k.a. Lady Mot ("mot" meaning "word" in French), is a native Calgarian, graphic designer, poet, and vocalist. Lady Mot began exploring the facets of spoken word poetry with her debut performance in the 2005 Calgary International Spoken Word Festival. Performance highlights: Calgary Stroll of Poets (2005), Liberate the Voice (2005), Wawapalooza Fundraiser for Ghanaian Youth Projects (2005), and Amnesty International Women's Rights Gala at the UofC (2006). She won the 2006 Canada Poetry Face-Off in Calgary.

A. Gregory Frankson, a.k.a. Ritallin, is an author, performer, speaker and arts educator based in Ottawa. Co-founder of the Capital Slam poetry series, he produced the *Live at Capital Slam* compilation CDs in 2005 and 2006. His EP recording *Capital Thoughts* and his debut book of poetry *Cerebral Stimulation* were released in 2006. Greg is Creative Director of Cytopoetics, providing creative services for business, education and the community.

Amanda Hiebert has been on the Toronto Slam team for each of the past six years, performing and competing across North America. She has performed over a hundred shows in the Greater Toronto Area and has been featured on CBC Radio's *Word Beat.* As a playwright, Amanda has written and produced two full-length plays. Her second play, a one-woman production titled *Confessions of a Girl Next Door,* was staged at the Havana Theatre to sold-out audiences and outstanding reviews. She is a member of spoken word collective Last Call Poets. She currently lives in Toronto with her wine rack.

kaie kellough is word sound systemizer. lit syncopator. resides in mo'real w/ wife kim. Lived in vncvr + clgry. authr lettricity <cumulus 04>. ed talking book <cumulus 06>. has contribd to cbc radio + tv. has dubbed + inked xcross xanada + u.s.a.

L.E.V.I.A.T.H.A.N., born and raised in Toronto, recorded a CD, *Enlightening with Lightening,* that was nominated for an Urban Music Association of Canada Award for Spoken Word Recording in 2005. He has performed on a Toronto slam team at the annual Canadian Festival of Spoken Word four times. He is currently working on *Runnin':- The Survival Series Double Album,* and is penning a science fiction novel about global warming.

Kevin Matthews lives, works and runs in Ottawa. He has performed his poetry in front of audiences around Canada – from hundreds to handfuls, and from symphonic concert halls to correctional facilities. Former Slammaster of the Winnipeg Poetry Slam, Kevin is a member of the Spoken Word Arts Network, the League of Canadian Poets, and part of the organizing crew for the Canadian Festival of Spoken Word.

Skip Stone (Jonathan Surla) is a native of Winnipeg, Manitoba, and made his spoken word debut when he competed with the city's team in the 2006 Canadian Festival of Spoken Word in Toronto. He again competed with the team at the 2007 CFSW. Stone is a member Winnipeg's Dangerous Goods b-boy crew and teaches b-boying, popping, and locking to youths at studios throughout the city. Email him at jaysurla@hotmail.com.

Magpie Ulysses has been a member of three Vancouver poetry slam teams, including two Canadian champion teams at the Canadian Festival of Spoken Word, competed in Vancouver's 2008 CBC Poetry Face-off, and has performed at festivals, poetry slams, fundraisers and house parties across Canada and throughout the United States. Magpie's work has been published in Common Ground Magazine, and two self-published chapbooks – *Tinfoil, Twist-ties & Other Shiny Things* and *Love poems from the aviary.*

RC Weslowski is a clown mouth gargling honey and juggling silly balls. His eyes are full of x-ray vision trying to get at the heart of things. RC has been involved with the Vancouver spoken word scene since 1997. He has performed at festivals across Canada including the Calgary International Spoken Word Festival and the Winnipeg Writers Festival. He has been on 5 Vancouver Poetry Slam teams including the 2006 CFSW National Champions. In 2007, RC finished 2nd at the World Cup of Poetry Slam in France. He has appeared in the dreams of people all around the world and may soon be coming to you.

The White Noise Machine is known for layered metaphor delivered in distinctively succinct staccato; alter ego Mike Smith is as enamoured with meditative page poems as with municipal politics, which he covers for *NOW Magazine.* Both have slammed at multiple Canadian Festivals of Spoken Word, and have appeared together on stages across Canada and the Midwest U.S. Rumours grow that they are actually just one man, speaking spiritually, puncturing politically, and humbled frequently by those he encounters on the way. His home is Toronto; his nation is poetry. His website is linebreaks.com.

Ardath Whynacht is a spoken word artist and member of Halifax's Word Iz Bond Collective. She has performed with beatboxers, musicians, contortionists, and kids across Latin America, Canada, and Australia. She won the Halifax CBC Poetry Face-off in 2006 and 2007 and is a veteran competitor at the Canadian Festival of Spoken Word. Her Halifax team won the national title in 2007.

Andrea von Wichert is a Winnipeg-based visual artist, writer and performer. She has competed at national poetry slams in Halifax and Toronto. Her story "On Maternal Death" won third prize in the 2007 McNally Robinson – Prairie Fire Short Fiction Contest, and was published in *Prairie Fire* magazine. She and collaborator Arlea Ashcroft have created the short films *Dead Mothers and Kitchen Floors* and *SNAPPERDOODLE – the Movie.* The latter will be presented as part of the 2008 Images Festival in Toronto.

Marquis Book Printing Inc.

Québec, Canada
2008